D1220951

HOW POLITICAL CAMPAIGNS AND ELECTIONS WORK

by Kevin Cunningham

Content Consultant
Dr. Arnold Shober
Associate Professor of Government
Lawrence University

Core Library

An Imprint of Abdo Publishing
www.abdopublishing.com

www.abdopublishing.com

Published by Abdo Publishing, a division of ABDO, PO Box 398166,
Minneapolis, Minnesota 55439. Copyright © 2015 by Abdo Consulting
Group, Inc. International copyrights reserved in all countries. No part of this
book may be reproduced in any form without written permission from the
publisher. Core Library™ is a trademark and logo of Abdo Publishing.

Printed in the United States of America, North Mankato, Minnesota
102014
012015

THIS BOOK CONTAINS
RECYCLED MATERIALS

Cover Photo: iStockphoto
Interior Photos: iStockphoto, 1, 8, 10, 25; iStock/Thinkstock, 4; Charles
Dharapak/AP Images, 7; Photos.com/Thinkstock, 12; Jupiterimages/
Thinkstock, 16; Louis Lanzano/AP Images, 21; Digital Vision/Thinkstock, 22,
28, 38, 45; Wilfredo Lee/AP Images, 31; Thinkstock, 34; Elise Amendola/AP
Images, 40

Editor: Heather C. Hudak
Series Designer: Becky Daum

Library of Congress Control Number: 2014944213

Cataloging-in-Publication Data
Cunningham, Kevin.
 How political campaigns and elections work / Kevin Cunningham.
   p. cm. -- (How the US government works)
ISBN 978-1-62403-633-0 (lib. bdg.)
Includes bibliographical references and index.
1. Political campaigns--United States--Juvenile literature. 2. Politics, practical-
-United States--Juvenile literature. 3. Voting--United States--Juvenile
literature. 4. Elections--United States--Juvenile literature. 5. United States--
Politics and government--Juvenile literature.   I. Title.
324--dc23
                                                           2014944213

We the People

insure domestic Tranquility, provide for the com
and our Posterity, do ordain and establish this

Article. I

CHAPTER ONE

The Separation of Powers

The United States is a representative democracy. This means US citizens vote for the people who serve in government. The men who established the government are known as the Founding Fathers. They believed the government would work best if it were split into three sections, or branches. This system is known as a separation of powers. It gives each branch a part of

The Constitution is the highest law in the country. It explains how the government works. It also lists the basic rights of all US citizens.

Political Parties

Political parties are large organizations. They are made up of politicians and supporters who share the same basic ideas. The Constitution does not mention political parties. In fact, George Washington disliked the idea of parties. He worried elected workers would work harder for their party than for all citizens. Most recent elections feature a candidate from the Democratic Party running against a candidate from the Republican Party.

governmental power. The Founding Fathers made sure each branch had ways to limit the power of the other branches. The responsibilities of the three branches are laid out in the US Constitution. This important document took effect in 1788.

The Branches

The legislative branch, or legislature, decides on new laws. The people elected to work for this branch may represent an entire state or a small part of a town. The federal legislature is called the US Congress.

The head of the executive branch often holds the power to cancel a law passed by the legislature. This type of power is known as a veto.

The executive branch leads a country, state, or town. Citizens often vote for and elect the head of the executive branch. The head of the executive branch in the federal government is the US president.

For some state courts, citizens directly elect judges. But not always. US presidents nominate candidates for the US Supreme Court. The Senate confirms the justices. Governors do the same in some of the states.

At the state level, governors are the head of the executive branch. Mayors head this branch in cities, towns, and villages. These leaders often have the power to choose the people who work in important government jobs.

US citizens can challenge laws passed by a legislature in a court of law. The judicial branch decides if the courts have applied a law in the correct way. The judicial branch also interprets the laws. They figure out if a person has broken a law and how that person should be punished.

FURTHER EVIDENCE

The Founding Fathers chose to split the government into three branches because of an idea they called the separation of powers. Investigate the separation of powers at the website below. Where did the idea come from? Why did the nation's founders include it in the US Constitution?

Separation of Powers

www.mycorelibrary.com/campaigns-and-elections

CHAPTER TWO

A New Kind of Government

In the 400s BCE, citizens of some cities in Greece began to allow groups of adult male citizens to vote on important city decisions. The voters' names were drawn at random. This system of government is called a direct democracy. It gives voters the power to directly affect government. But governing a large country like the United States needed a different kind of democracy.

The ancient agora of Athens, Greece, was a large, open space surrounded by buildings. Political meetings were held there.

The American Revolutionary War took place from 1775 until 1783. The 13 US colonies declared independence from Great Britain in 1776.

Governing the United States

After the American Revolutionary War ended in 1783, the Founding Fathers set up a new kind of government. They liked the system the ancient Greeks had set up. But they needed to adapt it to the United States. People lived too far from each other to get together to vote like the people of Greece did.

Instead, voters in the United States would elect someone from their area to represent them. This is called a representative democracy.

Getting Voters' Attention

People who run for election are known as candidates. They use campaigns to try to get people to vote for them. Campaigns are a series of actions candidates take in the months before Election Day. These actions may include holding rallies and giving speeches. The first campaign for the job of US president took place in 1796.

Predicting the Future

During an election, interviewers ask voters questions about candidates. These interviews are called polls. They help predict the likely winner of an election. In 1936, *The Literary Digest* mailed 10 million questionnaires to readers, asking whom they planned to vote for. The digest announced Alf Landon would win the election with 370 electoral votes. But Franklin Delano Roosevelt won with 523 electoral votes.

The Right to Vote

The United States did not always give all US citizens the right to vote. In the country's early years, typically only white, male property owners belonging to certain religious groups voted. Over time the law changed to include more people. By 1820, most states no longer had religious or property rules on voting. African-American males gained voting rights in 1868. In 1920 women won the right to vote. The law changed again in 1971 to make the voting age 18.

That year John Adams won the election for president. Thomas Jefferson came in second place and took on the job of vice president. Four years later, President Adams had become unpopular with US citizens. Jefferson was determined to take Adams's place. To try to win people over, Adams spoke directly to voters. Jefferson, meanwhile, remained at his Virginia farm. He let his supporters speak poorly of Adams in speeches and in newspaper stories. Adams lost the election of 1800. But his attempt to win set up a new way of running for office.

Political campaigns can sometimes become filled with rumors and name-calling designed to hurt the opposition. The Miller Center, a Presidential research institute, notes that this became especially fierce between Alexander Hamilton and John Adams in the election of 1800:

> A private letter in which Hamilton depicted Adams as having "great and intrinsic defects in his character" was obtained by Aaron Burr and leaked to the national press. It fueled the Republican attack on Adams as a hypocritical fool and tyrant. His opponents also spread the story that Adams had planned to create an American dynasty by the marriage of one of his sons to a daughter of King George III. According to this unsubstantiated story, only the intervention of George Washington, dressed in his Revolutionary military uniform, and the threat by Washington to use his sword against his former vice president had stopped Adams's scheme.
>
> Source: "The Campaign and Election of 1800." The Miller Center. The Miller Center, 2014. Web. Accessed October 1, 2014.

Changing Minds

Imagine you are an Adams supporter. How would you defend him from these attacks? Make sure you explain your opinion. Include facts and details that support your reasons.

REGISTER
HERE
TO VOTE

CHAPTER THREE

Roles and Representatives

Citizens across the country elect people to work as government officials. These jobs range from US president to members of boards who run libraries and school districts.

The US president heads the executive branch of the US government. This role is elected every four years. There are two major political parties that take part in presidential elections. They are the Democrats

The presidential election gets the most attention of all US elections.

and the Republicans. Each one chooses a candidate to run for president during an event called a convention. The nominees give speeches explaining what they will do for the country if elected. Then one nominee is chosen as the party's candidate for president.

The Electoral College

The Electoral College is a group of special voters called electors. Each elector represents one of the candidates running for president. People vote for the elector who supports the person they want to become president. The electors then place their vote for president and vice president. The candidate who wins the majority of electoral votes wins.

The Senate and the House

The legislative branch of the federal government has two houses, called chambers. They write laws. The upper chamber is the US Senate. Its members are called senators. Senators are elected every six

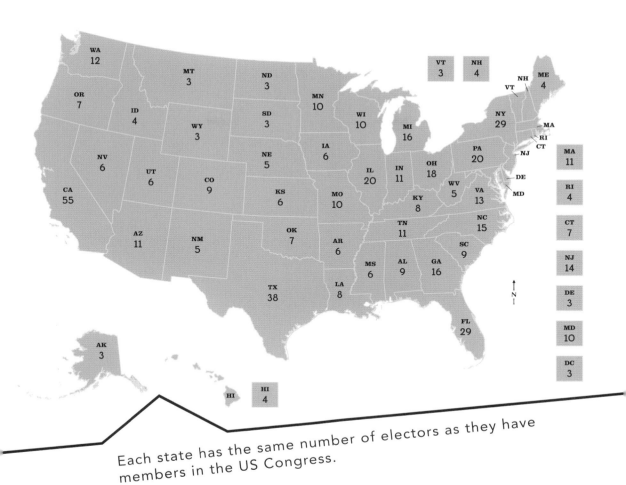

Each state has the same number of electors as they have members in the US Congress.

years. Voters in each state choose two senators to represent them.

The lower chamber is the US House of Representatives. Its members are called representatives. They are elected every two years. States with larger populations elect more representatives than states with smaller populations.

State Governments

Voters elect fellow citizens to the executive and legislative branches in the 50 states. In some states, members of the state judicial branch also campaign for their jobs.

A governor holds the chief executive office in a state. The person in this role appoints people for state jobs. Candidates for governor often run campaigns that last for months. They focus on issues that are important to voters across their state.

All state legislatures, except Nebraska, have two parts: the senate

Mapping Districts

Every ten years, state legislators use voter and census information to redraw the maps dividing voters into election districts. This is called redistricting. Sometimes the political party in charge redraws the map to give itself an advantage over the other parties. This is called gerrymandering. The party may try to pack all the opposing party's voters into a few districts. Or it may try to spread them out thinly into many districts. This gives the party the best chance to win in the most areas.

Andrew Cuomo was elected the 56th governor of New York in 2010.

and the state assembly or house of representatives. Nebraska's legislature has only one part. State legislatures consider and pass new laws. Candidates for offices, or seats, in a legislature most often represent a district. Each district has a certain number of voters. Lawmakers divide districts based on population, so a district's size can vary.

CHAPTER FOUR

Running the Campaign

Running for office takes energy, time, money, and a lot of help. In a local or county election, a candidate may depend on a handful of people as a campaign staff. A US Senate race requires dozens of paid staffers. Hundreds of people are needed to work on a campaign for US president.

Many people are involved in running a successful campaign.

Getting Started

Every campaign has a campaign manager. This person organizes the campaign staff and its tasks. Campaign managers often answer press questions. They also lend support to the candidates. The campaign manager is on the job around the clock.

A campaign needs a treasurer. This person oversees the campaign's money. The job requires honesty and an eye for detail. The treasurer must be willing to track down information about money, election laws, and other important facts.

Campaigns also need a fundraiser. This person finds people, groups, and businesses willing to donate money to help the candidate win the election. The fundraiser then connects the candidate to the donors. Fundraisers also come up with ideas to get the public to donate to the candidate. Concerts and auctions often bring in campaign dollars.

The fundraising team keeps detailed computer data and mailing lists. They use letters, phone calls,

Candidates may make contact with donors at a special dinner. Or they may contact them by phone, in a private meeting, or at a small gathering in a house.

and e-mails to contact possible donors throughout the campaign.

The volunteer coordinator finds and organizes the unpaid workers who give their time to a campaign. This person knows how to give clear, quick orders. A good coordinator sets schedules and matches volunteers to the best jobs for them.

The C&E Report

Campaigns have expenditures, or money used to purchase goods and services. Each candidate must file a Contributions and Expenditures (C&E) report with the Federal Election Commission or a similar state agency. This report shows how the campaign is spending its money. The opposing candidate's team looks at this report. They hope to find mistakes or money spent on items not meant for use in the campaign. If they do, they make sure reporters and voters learn about them. A good treasurer makes sure the campaign spends its money in the best ways possible. This ensures there can be no bad news stories.

Every campaign needs a communications director. This person helps share the candidate's ideas with the public. He or she may work with a team of volunteers or paid staff. This team spreads campaign messages through newspapers, the Internet, radio, and television. A candidate's Facebook page, Twitter feed, and blog are important parts of a campaign.

Online Messaging

Studies show about eight out of ten cell phone

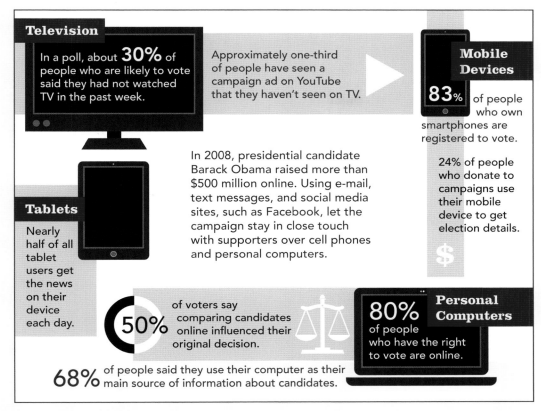

Television

In a poll, about **30%** of people who are likely to vote said they had not watched TV in the past week.

Approximately one-third of people have seen a campaign ad on YouTube that they haven't seen on TV.

Mobile Devices

83% of people who own smartphones are registered to vote.

24% of people who donate to campaigns use their mobile device to get election details.

In 2008, presidential candidate Barack Obama raised more than $500 million online. Using e-mail, text messages, and social media sites, such as Facebook, let the campaign stay in close touch with supporters over cell phones and personal computers.

Tablets

Nearly half of all tablet users get the news on their device each day.

50% of voters say comparing candidates online influenced their original decision.

80% of people who have the right to vote are online.

Personal Computers

68% of people said they use their computer as their main source of information about candidates.

Spreading the Word

Study this graphic showing the effect technology has on campaigns. How does the information presented compare to what you have learned from the text? How is it similar to what you have learned? How is it different?

owners vote. And nearly 70 percent of people say they use their computer as their main source of information about candidates. Social networks also let supporters talk with each other and plan events.

CHAPTER FIVE

On the Campaign Trail

The campaign team gets to work as soon as the candidate decides to run for office. The candidate, with help from the treasurer and campaign manager, must file forms with the state government saying he or she plans to run for office. The fundraiser draws up a plan to chart how much money the campaign will need to print signs, put up a website, and buy all the things a candidate needs.

The campaign prints signs for people to show their support for a candidate.

The communications team figures out how to present the candidate's ideas in a way that is easy for voters to understand.

Hit the Ground Running

In a campaign for a major office, the candidate announces his or her plan to run for election with a speech to supporters. The communications team tells the media about the event so they can cover it on TV and radio, as well as in newspapers and online.

In their speeches, candidates explain why they want to serve and what they plan to do if elected.

Campaigning

Running for a major office, such as president, governor, or US senator, is a full-time job.

Canvassing

Volunteers use lists of registered voters to find out where a candidate's supporters live. They may also make direct contact with people in the district. This is done by going door to door or by making phone calls. Political workers call this process canvassing.

There are times when long days and nights of campaigning take their toll. In 1992 Bill Clinton lost his voice. He had to stop working for a few days and cancel a major speech.

A candidate's day often starts before sunrise. First he or she might meet with the campaign manager to go over the day's activities. Another morning activity might be to call donors to ask for money.

After breakfast, a candidate may take part in an interview at a local TV or radio station. From there a car may take the candidate to a public place where he or she can shake hands and chat with voters. The candidate may then give a speech to a local club. Afterward he or she may go to a mall to meet more voters.

At lunchtime the candidate may visit a local diner. He or she can go from table to table shaking hands,

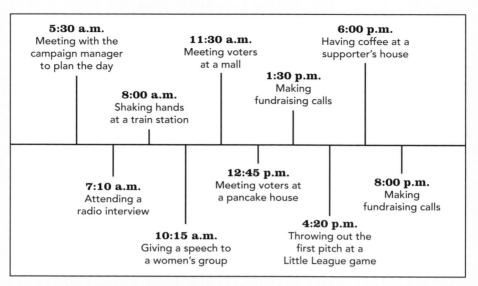

A Day in the Life of a Candidate

This schedule shows the many places a candidate might visit in a single day on the campaign trail. After reading about campaigns, what did you imagine it would be like? How has that idea changed?

taking pictures, answering questions, and asking for votes. Hungry or not, the candidate will likely have a meal. While running for president in 1999, George W. Bush stopped at Howard's Restaurant in Colebrook, New Hampshire. He even poured coffee for customers.

Meeting Voters

Candidates need votes from people of many different ages and backgrounds. The campaign staff schedules stops that bring the candidate in contact with all kinds of voters. Throwing out the first pitch at a Little League game introduces the candidate to parents. Elderly voters may meet the candidate at their nursing home. A trip to a nearby college lets the candidate meet students.

On the way home, the candidate might review the day with the campaign manager. Then the candidate returns to the campaign trail the next day.

EXPLORE ONLINE

Chapter Four focuses on a day in the life of a candidate on the campaign trail. One of the main goals of a campaign is to make people aware of the candidate. The website below offers examples of campaign materials, such as buttons and bumper stickers. How do supporters use these items to help a candidate? How do campaign materials use photos, art, words, and colors to show candidates in a good way?

Past Presidential Campaigns
www.mycorelibrary.com/campaigns-and-elections

Election Day

O n Election Day, citizens cast their votes for the candidates they support. In the days leading up to Election Day, candidates and workers work harder than ever to reach voters. Advertisements hit radio, television, the Internet, and newspapers. And the candidates appear nonstop at events.

Supporters make phone calls and write e-mails, tweets, and Facebook updates.

Who Won?

We often know the results of an election by midnight on Election Day. Sometimes, though, the voting results are too close to call. Election workers then recount the ballots. They need to double check the results. A recount can take days or weeks. In 2000 the votes were very close when Al Gore ran for president against George W. Bush. The recount went on for five weeks before it was announced George W. Bush would be the next president.

Day of Decision

Each state has its own election laws. In all states, you must be a US citizen age 18 years or older to take part in a major election. Some people, such as those who have committed certain types of crimes, may lose the right to vote.

In every state but North Dakota, a person must first register to vote. Registration often means showing photo identification, such as a driver's license, to prove the person is who he or she says. Then the person must fill out a form a few weeks before an election.

Some states allow people to register to vote on Election Day.

US citizens vote for president and many other offices on the Tuesday after the first Monday of November. Other elections may take place on other days or over a period of days. In some states, a person can vote by mail within a certain number of days of Election Day.

Voting

Each voter must go to a specific place to vote. It may be a church or school, for example. Voting places

GOTV

Get Out the Vote (GOTV) is the term used to describe efforts to get people to vote. A GOTV effort makes sure a candidate's supporters get to the voting booth to cast a ballot. In the 2012 presidential election, 57.5 percent of US citizens who were able to vote did so. State and local elections draw far fewer voters. The New York City mayor's election in 2014 only brought out about 24 percent of voters. The numbers are even lower when neither the president nor Congress is on the ballot. The voter turnout for Election Day in Kane County, Illinois, only reached 13.2 percent in 2011.

After getting registered, a voter typically casts his or her vote in secret.

open early so people can vote before work if they choose. They stay open until the evening.

Voters wait in line for their turn. Workers check for a voter's name on a list called a roll. Then the voter is given a list, or ballot. It shows all the elections taking place that day.

The voter takes the ballot to the voting booth. The booth is screened from the rest of the room. This lets people make their choices in secret. In some places, voters check a name on a piece of paper. Then they drop the paper in a locked box. When voting ends, workers count the ballots. Today most voters poke holes in punch cards or use touchscreens to make their votes. Computers then add the numbers.

The Decision Is Made

The candidate, the candidate's family, and members of the campaign gather to watch the results on television. Workers and volunteers gather at a hotel or other public place in hopes of celebrating a victory. In 2008 that place was Grant Park in

John McCain called Barack Obama after losing the 2008 presidential election. Then McCain gave a speech to his supporters from the Arizona Biltmore Hotel.

Chicago, Illinois. There Barack Obama spoke to 240,000 supporters after the results showed he had won the presidential election.

Campaigns are important parts of democracy in the United States. They give candidates and voters a chance to interact before the election. On Election Day, voters get to participate in government by casting votes for the candidate that best fits their vision for their nation, state, or local community.

Once the vote is final, the losing candidate contacts the winner to offer congratulations. This custom began in the presidential election of 1896. William Jennings Bryan contacted President William McKinley by telegram. McKinley replied. Their messages said:

> *Senator Jones has just informed me that the returns indicate your election, and I hasten to extend my congratulations. We have submitted the issue to the American people and their will is law. —W. J. Bryan*

> *I acknowledge the receipt of your courteous message of congratulations with thanks, and beg you will receive my best wishes for your health and happiness. —William McKinley*

> Source: William Jennings Bryan. The Second Battle or the New Declaration of Independence, 1776–1900. *Chicago: W. B. Conkey Company, 1900. Print. 335.*

What's the Big Idea?

Take a close look at these messages. What did Bryan mean in his final sentence? What important role does this type of statement play in a democracy? Why would two candidates end a fierce election campaign with such pleasant words?

400s BCE

Cities in ancient Greece allow male citizens to vote on major government decisions.

1776 CE

The 13 colonies declare independence from Great Britain.

1788

The US Constitution takes effect.

1896

Williams Jennings Bryan begins the tradition of the loser congratulating the winner of the presidential election.

1920

US women win the right to vote.

1971

The US grants 18-year-olds the right to vote.

1796

The first presidential election between members of different political parties takes place. John Adams runs against Thomas Jefferson.

1800

John Adams becomes the first presidential candidate to actively campaign for the office of president.

1868

African-American men gain the right to vote.

2000

George W. Bush defeats Al Gore for president after a vote recount that lasts five weeks.

2008

Barack Obama uses online fundraising and text messaging in his campaign for president.

2012

The presidential election draws 57.5 percent of voters.

Say What?

Studying campaigns and elections can mean learning a lot of new vocabulary. Find five words in this book that you've never heard before. Use a dictionary to find out what they mean. Then write the meanings in your own words, and use each word in a new sentence.

Why Do I Care?

You may not be old enough to vote, but that doesn't mean election results don't play a part in your life. How do decisions made by elected officials affect you at school or at home? How might officials decide what you learn and how to keep you safe? Use your imagination!

Surprise Me

Chapter Six discusses voting. The process of voting can be interesting and surprising. After reading this book, what two or three facts about voting did you find most surprising? Write a few sentences about each fact.

You Are There

This book discusses how candidates earn the trust of people living in the areas they represent. Imagine you are a voter. A candidate is giving a speech in your community to try to get your vote. What would make you trust the candidate?

GLOSSARY

direct democracy
the idea of every citizen
voting on every government
decision

Electoral College
a group of electors who vote
on the offices of US president
and vice president

executive branch
the branch of government
that leads a country, state, or
town and is responsible for
carrying out laws

gerrymandering
the process of dividing
electoral districts in a way
that favors one party over
another

judicial branch
the branch of government
that interprets and applies
laws passed by the legislative
and the executive branches

legislative branch
the branch of government
that discusses and votes on
new laws

rallies
large gatherings held to
support a political candidate

**representative
democracy**
the idea of voters electing
fellow citizens to represent
voters and their interests
in government

LEARN MORE

Books

De Capua, Sarah. *Running for Public Office*. New York: Scholastic, 2012.

Goodman, Susan E., and Elwood H. Smith. *See How They Run: Campaign Dreams, Election Schemes, and the Race to the White House*. New York: Bloomsbury USA Children's Books, 2008.

Wilson, Mike. *The Election Process*. San Diego, CA: Greenhaven Press, 2008.

Websites

To learn more about How the US Government Works, visit **booklinks.abdopublishing.com**. These links are routinely monitored and updated to provide the most current information available.

Visit **www.mycorelibrary.com** for free additional tools for teachers and students.

INDEX

ABOUT THE AUTHOR

Kevin Cunningham has published more than 60 books on topics such as diseases, Native-American culture, and natural disasters. He lives near Chicago.